A CROWN FOR BRANWEN

HARRI WEBB

A Crown For Branwen

GWASG GOMER
1974

First Impression - June 1974

SBN 85088 250 8

© HARRI WEBB 1974

Published with the support
of the Welsh Arts Council

Printed by
J. D. Lewis and Sons Ltd.
Gomer Press, Llandysul

Est etenim vester
nam quondam praelia vestra
vestrorumque ducum cecinit.

Geoffrey of Monmouth

ACKNOWLEDGMENTS

Many of the poems in this collection have appeared in the following magazines : *Poetry Wales, Planet, Anglo-Welsh Review, Welsh Nation, Second Aeon.*

' Never Again ' and ' MS found in a Bottle ' have been featured in the Welsh Arts Council's Dial-a-poem Service.

CONTENTS

PENNILLION

Colli iaith a cholli urddas
Colli awen, colli barddas
Colli coron aur cymdeithas
Ac yn eu lle cael bratiaith fas.

Colli'r hen alawon persain
Colli tannau'r delyn gywrain
Colli'r corau'n diaspedain
Ac yn eu lle cael clebar brain.

Colli crefydd, colli enaid
Colli ffydd yr hen wroniaid
Colli popeth glan a thelaid
Ac yn eu lle cael baw a llaid.

Colli tir a cholli tyddyn
Colli Elan a Thryweryn
Colli Claerwen a Llanwddyn
Â'r gwlad i gyd dan ddŵr llyn.

Cael yn ôl o borth marwolaeth
Cân a ffydd a bri yr heniaith
Cael yn ôl yr hen dreftadaeth
A Chymru'n dechrau ar ei hymdaith.

A CROWN FOR BRANWEN

I pluck now an image out of a far
Past and a far place, counties away
On the wrong side of Severn, acres
Of alien flint and chalk, the smooth hills
Stubtly, unmistakeably English, different,
I remember, as if they were China, Sinodun,
Heaven's Gate and Angel Down, the White Horse
Hidden from the eye of war, Alfred at Wantage,
His bodyguard of four Victorian lamp-posts
And his country waiting for another enemy
Who did not come that summer. Everything
Shone in the sun, the burnished mail of wheat
And hot white rock, but mostly I recall
The long trench.

      A thousand years from now
They'll find the line of it, they'll tentatively
Make scholarly conjectures relating it
To Wansdyke, the Icknield Way, Silbury.
They'll never have know a summer
Of tense expectancy that drove
A desperate gash across England
To stop the tanks.

      Most clearly I see
The tumbled ramparts of frantic earth
Hastily thrown up, left to the drifting
Seeds of the waste, and the poppies,
Those poppies, that long slash of red
Across the shining corn, a wound, a wonder.

Lady, your land's invaded, we have thrown
Hurried defences up, our soil is raw,
New, shallow, the old crops do not grow
Here where we man the trench. I bring
No golden-armoured wheat, the delicate dance
Of oats to the harvest is not for me nor
The magic spears of barley, on this rough stretch
Only the poppies thrive. I wreathe for you
A crown of wasteland flowers, let them blaze
A moment in the midnight of your hair
And be forgotten when the coulter drives
A fertile furrow over our old wars
For the strong corn, our children's bread.
Only, princess, I ask that when you bring
Those bright sheaves to the altar, and you see
Some random poppies tangled there, you'll smile,
As women do, remembering dead love.

SARABAND

The fire dancers flicker above the snow,
They steal along the edges of the night,
Tinkle their tambourines of utter cold
And hold aloft torches of icy flame,
Swirl pale, transparent draperies that fall
In silky folds about the tranced moon.

The silent dancers sway about the moon
Leaping and twirling on soft feet of snow
And as they soar the stars seen through them fall
Slowly and seem to slide out of the night
Until in a steep ebb of curtseying flame
They climb again each to its throne of cold.

The polar dancers limber in the cold,
Parade with soundless steps about the moon
A wavering palisade of airy flame
That throws no shadow on the still snow
Nor any lightening on the stark night
Where the ice whispers and white flakes fall.

The electric dancers swoop, flutter and fall
Down, down from the high to the lower cold,
Vanishing, leaving an abrupt black night.
Where are they gone ? Hiding behind the moon ?
Now there is only darkness, only snow.
Huge sudden space has swallowed the thin flame.

The ghost dancers are born again in flame,
Their shimmering battlements will never fall,
Tall towers sovereign over the snow
Unfurl and flaunt banners against the moon
Proclaim posession of the realms of cold
In proud carnival around the rim of night.

The zenith dancers are the queens of night
Veiled in white vesture of dalmatic flame,
Their pageant moves in triumph to the moon,
And tumbling constellations lurch and fall
In panic flight out to the furthest cold
While these command the conquered plains of snow.

Dancers of night, dancers over the snow
Of uncreated flame and pure cold,
    Dance till the moon fall.

POSTCARD FROM LLANRWST

I don't want another night like that again.
There were three of us in this room,
A small room, too, And a dog
Bought seventeen years ago for the gun
And still hunting rabbits in his sleep,
And all the weather in Wales pressed down
On the Conway valley, squeezing out thunder,
Lightning, heavy rain, the lot.
Wara teg though, the view was interesting.
Too interesting, if anything : the Gwydir Chapel
Window to window with us, almost.
It isn't everyone who can go to bed
With a full view of Llywelyn Fawr's coffin.
Next morning I went to pay my respects
To the empty sarcophagus.
There were also present
Two lawnmowers and a milking stool.

ABBEY CWMHIR

Cowpasture and the ragged line
Of a ruined wall. A few more cartloads
Of dressed stone filched for a new farmhouse
Or sections of clustered column taken for a cheesepress
And there would be nothing, less even
Than these scrappy remains under the big trees.
The coffin-lid of an old abbot is propped up
Behind the door of the Victorian church,
That's all. Heavy with July the elms
Remember nothing.

                  Appropriately
There is no signpost, not even a fieldpath
To the place where they brought the hacked trunk,
Who were they, I wonder, who lugged him here,
All that was left of him, after the English
Had done their thing, what went on in their minds,
Conventional piety, simple human pity
Or the cosmic grief the Son of the Red Judge
Sang into the stormwind, as they urged the pony
Felted with its winter coat, and over the crupper
The bloody carcase, along the bad ways ?

Centuries later, in high summer, I feel the cold.

ONE DAY

Tom the cowman, caked gumboots squelching
Cold mud, his stained old oilskin
Belted with binder-twine, with a rough-cut stick
To prod gently along the dripping lane
His herd to the milking-shed, walking at their walk,
One day
In an ironed overall may lead them
Into the ring, rosetted.

Bryn is still there after the others
Have packed up training, gone for a pint.
Light fails, thin drizzle falls, no-one is watching,
Only the posts, challenging, hostile
As he practises placekick after placekick.
One day
In a red shirt he may run
Out into the great roar.

Huw's light burns late, his coffee
Is a sour puddle, his eyes are aching.
Hunched at his desk, mocked, besieged
By screwed-up paper, he groans, curses.
Irritably he scratches out a word.
One day
His name called, he may stand
To wear a crown.

Wil on the doorstep, patient captive
Of a whined grievance, nods, soothes, makes notes
Shifts from one foot to another, runs through
In his mind the correspondence, the case-load,
Programmes, priorities, pamphlets.
One day
Out of all this
He will lead a people.

A TRUE STORY

The valley was drowned, the inhabitants
Properly compensated, decently re-housed.
The dam was opened by Her Majesty the Queen.
It was a popular decision at the time
To leave the stone-built village where it stood,
To leave the church and the church bells.
It would be nice, they said, to hear them
Ringing under the water, the bells
Of the drowned village.

After a few years, men went out in boats
And dynamited the steeple
To silence the bells.

This happened, oddly enough,
In England.

ENDS

Caesar lies dead, the skies rain fire,
The Tiber is in flood,
Rebellion stalks the streets of Rome,
The moon has turned to blood.

In an unknown, an unnamed land
Beyond an unknown sea,
Deep in the silence of the woods,
A leaf falls from a tree.

NEWS

When the wind is in the north
It rarely brings a thing of worth
When the wind is in the south
It blows the words out of your mouth
When the wind is in the east
It turns a man into a beast
When the wind is in the west
It's soft and warm like mother's breast.

FINE FEATHERS

Starling in your Persian armour,
Pigeon in your parson's grey,
Robin redbreast, cheeky charmer,
Sooty sparrow, flashing jay . . .
Bourgeois blackbird, dressed the neatest
Of all the birds my garden throng,
You because your tune is sweetest
Shall lead them in the loyal song.
Sweetest, strongest, swiftest, shiniest,
Fan your feathers, bob beak-down
And hail your king, though he's the tiniest,
The wren that wears the golden crown.

GENERATION GAP

When I was young and serious
About the land I went
And heard no song to cheer me
In Gower or in Gwent.

Now I'm too old for weeping,
And happier every hour
To hear the song that's sweeping
The land from Gwent to Gower .

FOR THE WELSH SCHOOL AT CWMBRAN

Silver Wye and Severn gold
A town that's new, a tongue that's old
Let the ancient truth be told.

Rome and all her eagles go
Where an empire's pride lies low
Cocks of Croesyceiliog crow.

Gwent is green and Llwyd the grey
Our river's called, but so they say
It was Stonebreaker in its day.

Where our history casts its spell
Let Llantarnam's ruins tell
How the fighting abbot fell.

Children you whose days shall see
Another empire's end, and we
Who once were bound, walking free,

Ours to tend the flowers that grow
In the valley of the crow
Let the sweeter music flow.

THE SINGER
(*For Heather Jones*)

A young girl sings
A grief that's old
A young voice rings
New-minted gold.

A sweet voice sings
A bitter pain
Healing as spring's
Clear cool rain.

Old splendid things
New tender tales
A slim girl sings
Her song fills Wales.

TO A READER

Yes, you have heard, and turned away
Unheeding from the songs I've sung.
For you my tunes have had their day
And I am dead and you are young.

Your's is the country I would see
Beyond my age's endless night,
Half-heedless of its liberty
That's your's by custom and by right.

And there, maybe, on some dark shelf
Or in a tedious book at school
Lingers a little of myself
For you to smile at as a fool

Who wasted all his scanty powers
Harping on grudges, hopes and wrongs,
And you will say, He's none of ours,
Today we sing far different songs.

Let it be so, and I am glad.
I only sang of what I knew,
Your world is bright where ours is sad
And what are all our griefs to you ?

And so you throw my book aside,
A tale of best forgotten days,
You who are free and walk in pride.
For me, it is a form of praise.

HARRI WEBB TO HARRI VAUGHAN

Yours was a light I do not see
And do not seek to find,
Wisdom you sought, and mystery
That are not to my mind.

Under the same Silurian sky,
Though centuries fall between,
We gaze and wonder, you and I,
At all that's to be seen.

For you, these waters, earth and air
In heavenly splendour shone,
For me the glory they declare
Is in themselves alone.

To you our rivers sang of bliss
Beyond all mortal pales,
I ask no other heaven than this,
My paradise is Wales.

Yet still I stretch to you a hand
And look you in the eyes,
Who share the same enchanted land,
The same all-healing skies.

BRIEFING

Come down from the high horse. For a space let him canter
With tossing mane over the mountains. This is a job
That must be finished on foot, with a short knife.
So prop the glittering lances, doff the plumes
At the cave's entrance. It is low and threatening.
You must bend your head, crouch, inch into the darkness
Until you get the feel of the foul place. Then
By his stink you'll trace him. Remember the long tribute.
Remember, too, a liberation
Is also a suicide.

Dodge the quick horns and hooves and bewildering breath.
In the dead end of the administrative labyrinth no precise
Instructions apply. But when the moment comes
You'll know well enough.
They're tough these old monsters and take a lot of finishing.
It won't be easy but it's either him or us.
And in any case, you won't be the same afterwards.
In a sense you've nothing to worry about, just as long
As you can live till the bright moment of emergence
And hold the reeking beast head up
In the caparisoned noonday where the high horse waits.

PENYDARREN PARK

Here where the legions shuffled to a halt,
Grounded their spears on the furthest dust
Their sandals ever trod, stood at ease,
Gobbed, swore and grumbled, dug their fort,
Foraged, got drunk, played dice,
Chased the wild white-skinned women,
Dreamt of home, brought three centuries
Of uneasy peace, called it a day, struck camp
And handed over to the cowboy princes
And their mad harpists, are the bungalows
Of my neighbours and friends. The tell me
However hopefully they dig their gardens
They never find any remains.

ACQUAINTANCE

Knew Twynog, dimly remembered
Creidiol, could tell you the exact house
In Overton Street where Myfyr Emlyn
Was inspired to write Yr Hen Gerddor,
Referred to Sir John and Lady Charlotte
As if he had known them personally,
Could recite by heart the rollcall
Of the hundred pubs between Pant Cadifor
And the Bont, and accurately mimic
The four separate accents from the Bont
To Penywern, had prayed with Evan Roberts,
Booed Pritchard Morgan, cheered Keir Hardie,
Sung under Dan Mochwr, got drunk
At Ffair y Waun, taken to the mountain
To avoid call-up, hailed S. O. Davies
The new Mezziah, knew the circumstances
Of Twm Pwdin's murder. We called him
Dai Dowlais. He is dead now.

WHERE ?

My cousins, dark men, crammed with me
Into the stoneflagged bar, the low ceiling
An imminent hangover inches above our heads,
The atmosphere as impenetrable as the dialect.
It was the day of the races, red faces shone
Through thick blue smoke, loud talk
Banged down from the beams, bounced off the bottles
Behind the bar, rang from the glasses, tinkled
Around a massive iron poker and brass shovel
Gleaming in the blackleaded fireplace,
The yawning gateway to the Other Realms.
Jammed into a highbacked settle of ancient wood
Polished by generations of boozers' backsides,
We sweated beer, rocked forward laughing
At jokes we could hardly hear, leaned back
Sated, sodden. Through a small green window
A low steep hill, one of a special breed
Like the sheep and ponies on it, grinned in at us.
Behind its heaving shoulder a famous tide
Sparkled with sewin. Out there, somewhere,
Olwen walked through the woods, trailing trefoils.
We never saw her. Nor the races, either.
My cousins, dark men, knew the results beforehand.

A VOICE IN THE WIND

The wind blows in old memories like dead leaves,
Inconsequential, tumbling, then one sticks
Tapping, tapping, impossible to dislodge,
Places, names, none of them somehow quite
The expected visitor. They've been there all the time
Whirling about in the dark, now they won't go,
Tapping, tapping, names, memories.
The wind in my roof tonight blows in from the Waun Pound,
High common above three valleys crammed
With small houses and huge wrongs, the air
Brisk, the northern crop of the coal-measures,
Abrupt frontier between slagheaps and rough pasture.
That's where I saw you, heard you, shook your hand.
Our paths touched an instant, that was all.
You stood on the back of a lorry, spoke to a crowd
Of perhaps a thousand, a politician in a smart suit,
Master of oratory, at home, confident, in command,
The world was listening. Unconsciously I noted
Your back was turned to the hills, you gestured
Always to the valleys below. You spoke of a dream,
Summoning your people—yes, they were your people,
Yours, and you were their leader, you held them
In the hollow of your hand—to build anew
Where the old tyrants had cheated and despoiled.
The crowd was silent. It could have been a scene
Anytime in our history, the chieftain aloft
And the host mustered to follow.

Already though,
It was something of a sentimental pilgrimage,
The spot chosen because here in the starving years
The gaunt contingents had converged from Rhymni,
Tredegar, Ebbw Vale, the Valleys of the Shadow,
To seek a dawn, and even on that day
Of sunshine and solidarity, there was somehow
The breath of premonition that all too soon
There would be no more such meetings, nor no man
Like this one to inspire them, and the people
Would have found other places to go, the Waun Pound
As unregarded as before the first forges
Flamed in Gwent. Here and there in the crowd
The older men whispered this behind their hands
And drew their belted raincoats closer around them.
But I will not begrudge you or myself the bright memory
Of Aneurin Bevan standing against the sky,
A Silurian prince, even though you lost your way.

THAT SUMMER

The first thing I remember is the General Strike,
My father in his shirtsleeves leaning on the front gate
Smoking his pipe in the sunshine,
Miss Davies the shop calling across to him,
Are you out, Mr. Webb ? I hear now
Her bright amused voice, see Catherine Street
Empty and clean, hear the nine days' silence
As the last ripple of a lost revolution
Ebbed into history and the long defeat
Began to mass its shadows. The ambulances
Were absent from the road beside the hospital,
Garn Goch Number Three, Great Mountain, Gilbertsons,
Elba, the names I learnt to read by, names
Of collieries and tinworks, names of battlefields
Where a class and a nation surrendered
The summer they killed Wales.

We spent the time on the sands, played all day.
We had the whole place to ourselves,
Or so it has always seemed, from the West Pier
To Vivian Stream. When you are five years old
There are things you understand more easily
Than ever afterwards, that the sea is huge
And goes on for ever from Swansea, the moon
And the hospital clock inhabit the same sky,
Neighbours. But there are other things, and these
You only understand later, much later.
Inland, in those ambulance villages, the other side
Of Town Hill, from stations further up the line
From Mumbles Road, already it was beginning,

The losers' trek, the haemorrhage of our future.
But for a child there is only the present.
Dad, I said, there'd be lovely if the strike
Was all the time, then you and me could come
Down the sands every day and play. He laughed.
It wouldn't do, son, he said, it wouldn't do,
There's got to be work, see, there's got to be work.
Chasing a ball I didn't stop to argue, forgot
I'd ever asked the question till later, long after
The summer my country died.

CHINOISERIE

Ceramic Zoroastrian funerary urns,
Zoophorm lamps and copper coins pierced
After our fashion inform us of the Sogdians,
Immigrants to the left bank of the Chu
From the mysterious west, the kingdoms
Of engineers and jugglers. They have brought
To Lo-Yang their wonderful merchandise :
Golden peaches the size of a goose's egg,
The horses of Ferghana, coloured glass
And supple iron armour, but above all
We praise their most precious import, the Vine.
By Lop-Nor and all over the west
Their cities are vineyards and orchards
Glowing with grapes, ablaze with cherryblossom.
They drink the wine of grapes, but we prefer
To eat the fruit. We get drunk decently
As gentlemen should, on rice-spirit, like our fathers,
The sound traditional beverage that inspired
Li-Po to gather moonbeams from the river
(Always a mistake to mix spirits with water)
Now as we sit in this exquisite pavilion
Nibbling the purple grapes, we set ourselves
A subtle philosophical problem : is it better
To eat the fruit or drink the wine ? Which
Is the higher wisdom ? The lives
Of how many poets have been saved ?

NEVER AGAIN

You never saw such a stupid mess,
The government, of course, were to blame.
That poor young kid in her shabby dress
And the old chap with her, it seemed such a shame.

She had the baby in a backyard shed,
It wasn't very nice, but the best we could do.
Just fancy, a manger for a bed,
I ask you, what's the world coming to?

We're sorry they had to have it so rough,
But we had our troubles, too, remember,
As if all the crowds were not enough
The weather was upside-down for December.

There was singing everywhere, lights in the sky
And those drunken shepherds neglecting their sheep
And three weird foreigners in full cry—
You just couldn't get a good night's sleep.

Well now they've gone, we can all settle down,
There's room at the inn and the streets are so still
And we're back to normal in our own little town
That nobody's heard of, or ever will.

And though the world's full of people like those,
I think of them sometimes, especially her,
And one can't help wondering. . though I don't suppose
Anyone will ever know who they were.

DAY OUT

Up the Golden Valley
Sunday afternoon
Kenderchurch and Michaelchurch
Michaelmas is soon

Up the Golden Valley
Season nearly done
Every ripening apple
Is a golden sun

Up through Ewyas Harold
Stop at Abbey Dore
Admire the church restored by
Viscount Scudamore

Where the road climbs steeply
Pause and view the scene
Woods and fields and orchards
Down to Bredwardine

Dorstone, Bacton, Vowchurch
At the end of day
Peterchurch and Cusop
Cup of tea at Hay

Cabalva, Clifford, Clyro
Where the Wye-mist swirls
The ghost of Parson Kilvert
Is chasing little girls

Huge against the sunset
Hills of home stand stark
Gently now on Ewyas
Dewfall, dusk and dark

Back in Monday Merthyr
Work must still be done
Golden Golden Valley
Apples in the sun.

THE MEETING

You couldn't have got much further up the valley,
The hills behind us were a steep green wall
And all the folk were talkative and pally
As they crowded to the meeting at the hall.

We're very glad to see you here, they told us,
We don't get many coming from outside,
As they steered us past the potholes, sheep and boulders,
The most interesting thing since Mabon died.

The schoolroom where we spoke was neat but dowdy,
The chairman knew the people all by name,
The heckling, on the whole, was not too rowdy,
They knew the rules and they enjoyed the game.

And then, under the stars, it somehow started
As the audience drifted to the street outside
As to and fro the dialectic darted,
For some where for and some against the Blaid.

Long-tethered tempers rose like boiling custard,
The quarrel echoed from the high dark hill,
Young men were passionate and old men blustered,
The girls, alas, were vehement and shrill.

And some who saw us off were rather nettled.
We don't know why you've come here, for a start.
Before tonight we were all nicely settled,
Now you've gone and blown the bloody place apart.

THE NEXT VILLAGE TO MANAFON

It was half past seven on Saturday night
When we stopped off at the Powys Arms.
Already the locals were half-way tight,
Red-faced men from the steep green farms.

Some talked of girls and country pleasures
And some were grumbling about the hay
And some were discussing the bardic measures,
Heirs of Owain Cyfeiliog they.

We kept our end up, passing strangers,
As best we could, with what tales we knew,
Avoiding the subtle verbal dangers
Laid like poachers by the deft-tongued crew.

Song for song we joined in the singing
And not for a moment the clonk did flag,
The glasses clinked and the room was ringing.
I hope God drinks, said the village wag.

It was half-past nine on Saturday night
As we broke the spell and drove over the hill.
They pressed us to stay, but we took our flight
And none too soon, or we'd be there still.

THE MEDIUM IS THE MESSAGE

Belshazzar was an Eastern King
Who used to feast like anything.
His banquets, which went on and on
Were all the talk of Babylon,
Till, on the palace wall one night
A moving finger began to write :

Hands off the Hittites !
      Ban the Bow !

Baal is Dead !
      The Horse must go !

And other sentiments progressive,
The diners found it most depressive,
The King, to whom all this was new,
Dropped dead.

      I'm not surprised. Are you ?

Under the Bo-tree the Buddha sat
With his arms like this and his legs like that,
Achieving mystical exaltation
By inhibiting his circulation.

On top of old Smoky, in rotten weather,
Moses, at the end of his tether,
Was impressed by what he thought he heard,
Came rolling down the mountain with the Word.

To the sands of the desert the Prophet fled
Listening to noises inside his head,
Took down from dictation Allah's writ
While building up to a nasty fit.

While on the road to Damascus Paul
Seems to have had a most painful fall,
Was dazzled by the sun's hot glare
And saw a man who wasn't there.

He wasn't there again today
And now he'll never go away.
The moral of all this, dear brother,
Is : facts are one thing, truth another.

AND WHO'S LITTLE DOG ARE YOU?

In droving days my work earned praise
Twixt fair and market and carouse,
Coursing along the droving ways
And snapping at the heels of cows.

Though changed the time and changed the clime
I still can mind my whys and hows,
As popular as ever, I'm
Still yapping at the heels of cows.

ADVICE TO A YOUNG POET

Sing for Wales or shut your trap
All the rest's a load of crap.

RURAL DEVELOPMENT

The sheepruns are old memories,
Fallen the tuneful farmstead's walls.
Now all the trees are Christmas trees
And all the harvest glittering balls.

THOUGHTS IN AN AREA OF OUTSTANDING NATURAL BEAUTY

You haven't lived, they said to me,
Until you've seen our hills, our sea,
Our mountains strong from age to age,
Our fortress and our heritage.
So, dutifully here I stand
To view the splendours of our land,
The castled crag, the fabled shore,
So now I've lived, and I'd say more :
Until you've known this shame, this stress,
This beauty that is meaningless,
That's bought and sold on every side,
You haven't lived—you haven't died.

MISSIONARY POSITION

Let us give thanks, people of Wales
That we are raised so high above the nations
And are so blessed that we can afford
To scatter blessing broadcast. Take for example
The simple pagans of the Southern seas
Who, so astounded by the multiplicity
Of marvellous goods that come by ship and plane
Resembling nothing in their primitive culture
Have in their blindness made these things their god
Whom to bring down to dwell among them, they go in
For rigorous ascetic practices, or indulge
In wild ecstatic ceremonies, regrettably
Subversive of established order, but most often
They are to observed in senseless mimicry
Of white men's actions, building radios
Out of old boxes with no works inside
To summon the gods of cargo, marching up and down
Like soldiers, but to nowhere in particular,
Simply, and vainly, to obtain possession
Of artefacts whose manufacture is beyond
Their limited comprehension. People of Wales,
There's lovely it is, isn't it, that we
Are not a bit like that.

CONTINENT ISOLATED

There was a Fog in our pub the other night.
He trailed his native element with him. Fog
Came out of his ears, when he opened his mouth
What came up was pure Fogspeak. He discussed
At length and in detail his illnesses, and his wife's
Illnesses, and his wife's relatives' illnesses,
All caused, of course by fog, and the fate of
His country, dear old Fogland. As he denounced
The politicians, fog oozed out of his boots. Too soft,
He reckoned, to Frogs and Wogs. We Fogs
Do all the slog, he said, not like them slobs,
All they can do is snog and flog grog, can't
Even build a decent bog, the Frog. As
For good old fogfood, nothing like it, bacon
And fog for breakfast, fog and chips, and
Don't forget, none of them foreigners have got
A Royal Foggily. As he went out
All the foghorns sounded for him on the other side.

EIFIONYDD

Far from the scowl of progress,
From drab industry afar,
There's a land of sea and wildness
That bears no stain nor scar
Save where the hillside plough lays bare
The sweet spring earth in the mountain air.

Far from the idiot violence
Where wry new worlds repine
Here is the dawnworld's fragrance
That lingers like old wine,
Old, old, the murmuring voice that dreams
About Rhoslan between two streams.

And Lôn Goed's a green heaven
Where quiet is complete
From its roof of branches woven
To the soft grass at my feet,
It leads to nowhere, the leafy lane
But none who linger there complain.

Ah, sweet to be arriving
In that secluded vale
Far from the scenes of striving
And a world that's known and stale.
Alone I'd gladly wander there,
Or one with me, that peace to share.

                    (From the Welsh of R. Williams Parry)

BLUE BELLS

They come with the cuckoo's coming
And when she goes they die,
The wild and memoried fragrance,
The enchantment of the eye,
They come to us, they leave us,
Why must they say goodbye ?

Down in the woodland hollows,
The cliffs' steep flanks along,
On all but harrowed plowland
By field and hedgebank throng
The blue flowers of the springtime
That grow to the cuckoo's song.

From Llandegai church steeple
Sweet chimes the close of day
But far more sweetly swaying
The silent bells of May
That fill the mind with singing
And they must fade away.

For soon in nights of summer
And honeysuckle spells
The nightingale's carrillon
Its frequent story tells
And the wind holds no memory
Of the cuckoo or her bells.

(From the Welsh of R. Williams-Parry)

A MESSAGE HOME

Fly to Wales, my little songbird,
Take a message will you please
From this place of wrath and carnage
To the land of song and peace.
Though here Struma's running sweetly
In the moonlight as of yore,
You'd forget it all completely
If you'd seen the Menai shore.

And how will you be knowing
The place that you must greet ?
Fly till you see the mountains
With the waters at their feet,
Where the summer lingers longest,
Where the air is fresh and free,
Where the sea and sky are clearest,
That's Wales, my heart's country.

Fly till you find an island
Where you need no longer roam,
Where the cuckoo's song is earliest,
You'll be welcome, you'll be home.
Fly northward from Brynsiencyn
Do not dawdle by the Tŵr
And make your nest in Traffwll
In the garden of Glan Dŵr.

It's a garden full of blossom,
No fairer garden grows,
And there you'll meet with someone
Who is fairer than a rose.
Sing my sadness, sing to Megan,
Sing as sweetly as you may,
Sing till she feels the hiraeth
That burns my heart away.

And will you tell my cousin
I'd give the world for half an hour
To go fishing in the Traffwll
Far from the sound of war.
Together we'd go rowing
In the quiet starlight then,
Me with Megan and beside him
The girl from Allwadd Wen.

Once you'd sung to Wil and Megan
You'd want to stay, I'm sure.
Who'd come back to Macedonia
From the garden of Glan Dŵr ?

(From the Welsh of Cynan)
(1895-1970)

THE BAFFLED BIRDWATCHER
(*Diweirdeb Merched Llanbadarn*)

Talk about chocker, I could spit.
To hell with all the judies here,
I'm randy and can't get a bit.
Will they drop 'em ? No bloody fear.
I can't cop on to a fancy chick,
I can't find a frustrated wife,
Not even a boiling-piece who'll click,
They all must think I'm tired of life.
If only a bird would agree to go
For a nice little walk up to the wood
Dafydd would soon put on a show
That would do us both a bit of good.
I've always had a one-track mind
Like Garwy and that hot-arsed crew,
There's never a day I'm not inclined
To have a jump or maybe two.
I've tried to pick one up at mass
Each Sunday with my back to God
And my eyes skint for a likely lass
But they leave me strictly on my tod.
I'm togged up in my sharpest gear,
There's not much talent that I miss,
But one says in another's ear,
"Look at that stuck-up long-haired ciss,
There's one I wouldn't let get too close,
He's dangerous, he's bedroom-eyed,
I know the tricks of blokes like those".
And says the other by her side,
"I'd never let him above my knee,

He can go and jump into the lake".
See what the ravers think of me ?
I've had as much as I can take.
So here I am, I'm nackered, sunk,
I'll give it up as from today.
I know what, I'll be a monk—
No, I'll join the F.W.A.
I've had a right come-uppance, aye,
I'm packing up, retired sick,
This here's one scene that I'll pass by,
Where I never got to dip my wick.

(Somewhat after the Welsh of Dafydd ap Gwilym)

THE WOODS OF CYNON

Aberdare, Llanwynno, all
Merthyr and Llanfabon,
The worst thing ever to befall
Was cutting the woods of Cynon.

They cut down many a parlour sweet
So pleasant with the sun on,
Places where men and boys would meet
In the forest of Glyn Cynon.

If a man had to take flight
From vengence of the alien
He'd get a lodging for the night
With the nightingales of Cynon.

Many a birch tree in green attire
(Hanged high be every Saxon)
Is heaped as fuel for the fire
By the black men of iron.

For cutting down and making bare
The wild birds' resting place
May confusion be the share
Of the false English race.

Better should the English be
Hanged in the depths of ocean
In hell to dwell in misery
For cutting the woods of Cynon.

I heard them saying yesterday
The parish is now so dreary
All the red deer have gone away
To the black wood of Mawddwy.

Hunting the badger and the hind
And the roebuck in the dell
All that is now behind
For Cynon Woods are felled.

If a stag was in the chase
Before the huntsman running
You'd never see him slack his pace
Till he reached the woods of Cynon.

If a girl came, fairest fair,
Beside the river strolling,
Pleasant it was to meet her there
Down in the woods of Cynon.

And if they seek as in old days
For wood to bridge the river
Or build a church or a dwelling place
Glyn Cynon is no giver.

In judgment I'd set up a court
Of every honest fowl
And in his robes of office there
Their hangman be the owl.

If anybody asks who made
This cruel declaration,
It's one who often met his maid
In the forest of Glyn Cynon.

(From the Welsh of an Anonymous
17th Century Poet)

BI-CENTENARY

Cut daffodils, the topography
Of the Lake District, Batsford's
English Countryside in Ektachrome,
Anthologies, tight little bunches
Of cut lyrics wilting. Lives
By eminent scholars. This is
The two-hundredth anniversary
Of William Wordsworth, poet,
Ancient Monument, valuable asset
To the tourist industry, indispensable
Ingredient in Education, conditioning
Town kids to think that poetry
Is all about clouds, cuckoos
And bloody daffodils. Stale
From overexposure, the words
Will not come alive. I do my best,
It's no good, they've got him.
Here lies William Wordsworth
Killed by colour-supplements,
Murdered by thesis, buried
Under a cairn of footnotes
Piled high and heavy to keep under
The shouting madman, the seer,
The stranger, priest of darkness.

THE EMIGRANTS

They started walking from Llanbrynmair,
Men going ahead, women and children following,
To Carmarthen quay, but were warned in time,
The press gang are in town. The men turned east
And walked to Bristol. The women and children
Boarded ship, were wrecked on Llansteffan sands.
Stumbling ashore, they too turned east, walked to Bristol.
Some died. When at last they set sail
They were six stormy weeks at sea.
Landing, they resumed their walk : the length of Pennsylvania
Over the Alleghenies through the Cumberland Gap
To the headwaters of the Ohio. Down the Great Valley then
On rafts, made fast to the bank each night, until
They came to Paddy's Run. Frenchmen (where was Paddy ?)
Welcomed them, pressed them to stay. No,
They must walk yet further, Kentucky was waiting.
Evansville, Hopkinsville, Owensboro,
Tall corn, deep grass, land that grew everything
Except landlords. Next morning, though, their rafts were gone,
The moorings cut in the night. They stayed. They had to.
On those luminous plains there are thirty gathered churches
Where the gods of Wales are worshipped. Once a year
They have a Gymanfa Ganu and good luck to them.
One only asks, hearing the tale told,
Why did they have to walk so far ?
In the name of all their gods and ours,
What were they walking away from ?

WALES 1970

(*To my friend John Jenkins imprisoned for ten years in Wormwood Scrubbs, London.*)

Blinding unutterable unrestrained clamant
Entire starry close transparent
Snowy fugitive innumerable distant
Incessant unhoped-for despised jubilant
Feverish captive torn radiant
A land heavily pregnant.

(From the Breton of Paol Keineg)

MARWNAD FOR DRUMS

Low sky, grey sky, December sky,
But the time has passed
For mourning the dead.
It's raining, children,
Must we leave the dead
To bury the dead ?
No, children, no !
Our dead shall be buried
By our own hands, our own living hands
In living earth
Where we have sown the seed.

Memory is living, growing,
Their blood has dried on the walls
And in the streets of death
And on their murderers' hands.
Their blood is a voice that remembers,
And your blood, our murdered brothers,
Is ours who live.

What do you think we are, gentlemen ?
Do you think we are big kids
With short memories and ready smiles ?
That we are men on our knees ?

If only you knew, murderers,
That on each grave we have placed
three stones.

You know
stone is imperishable.
On each stone we have placed
Three red roses
Terrifyingly alive red roses
Alive like memory
Alive like blood
Alive like stone.

(From the Martiniquais of Auguste Macouba)

FOR FRANZ FANON

Bronze hero against the sun
Reined his horse to a prance,
Balanced and splendid
(But what had he done ?)
An attitude of France.
Bronze skins against carved stone
Crouching in rags and sweat,
Beating the ages away on a drum
Africa sits, in wait.
The Opera in the square,
Has plaques on its facade,
Florid phrases declare
Cervantes and Regnier
Were slaves and prisoners here.
This was Algiers then.
Everywhere tricolours hang
On s'en fout des indigènes
Sales gens, ils sont bons pour rien.
Up in the hills, in the *bled*
Poplar and white wall,
And rooves of Roman red
Extend Cezanne's Provence,
No doubt about it at all
This is clearly France.
Where the boulevard became
The road to the empty sands
Chiselled phrases proclaim
Mission civilisatrice.
The *colons* of rich lands
For whom life was sweet

Privileged and serene
Saw no end to the long peace
Nor the coming of their dark.
I often think of the scene
As I walk in St. Mary Street
As I walk in Cathays Park.

NOW

I never saw King Arthur waiting for a bus
Nor Gwenhwyfar shopping in the supermarket,
The wisdom of Myrddin is not obvious in the newspapers
And the wildest boar is safe from Kulhwch now ;
As for Olwen she's somehow lost the knack
Of coaxing the spring flowers to grow in her footprints,
Kai will eat and drink with the best of them
Down at the club but Gwalchmai and that lot
Have hared off somewhere and haven't been heard of
For a long time now. But there's one of them
Who's still very much with us. Yes, you've guessed,
It's Medrawd.

Why, hello ! Charming weather lately.

Memory, that old anarchist, keeps no rules,
Is no respecter of conventional wisdom. Memory
Is a gatecrasher, a dirty joker, a death's head.
For instance, all my recollections of the Holy Land
Should be, well, not exactly holy, but at least
Respectable, part of a pattern, bearing some relation
To the Good Book or Current Affairs. Deep down
Perhaps some potent apocalypse is still brewing
But somehow I hope not. It is better this way,
With all my memories rather disreputable—
Getting pissed in the Palestine Police Barracks
The Stern Gang later blew up—or wildly farcical
Like that Sunday on Haifa quay when a Bishop
Preached to the Second Cruiser Squadron, drawn up
All blanco and bullshit with our scruffier mob
The Fifth Destroyer Flotilla, all boiled raw
In the stinking heat, his asinine Anglican accent
Nagging God like a public school prefect. His sermon
Was about Origen. How he went on as we sweated
And craved for our grog. You'd have thought, really,
That Celsus was a paid up Obergruppenfuhrer.
He didn't tell all the truth about him, though,
That he'd cut off his balls to make sure of being holy.
Perhaps it was just as well, given the congregation,
I don't somehow think they'd have seen the point.
Yes, my memories are true ones. I avoided
All shrines, tombs, temples, pilgrimages,
Was resolutely profane, chose to take my liberty
In Tel Aviv, on the beach and in the nightclubs
Rather than the other places. Anyway, we all wanted out.

The dour drab Jews meant just as much to us
And just as little, as the picturesque Arabs.
Let the fuckers fight it out themselves, we said.
Even then our money was on Moshey. Jack was wiser
Than those set in authority over him.

                    (Years later
I saw, in a newsreel, Haifa docks again,
An old man with a long beard, straight off the boat
Knelt down and kissed the railway lines. Talk about laugh.)
Raffish memories, welcome like old mates.
Once you were not mere shades, but life itself.
Asserting against all history's prestige
That everything begins now, from where you are.
I think, too, as we gossip together a little
Before you scamper back to wherever it is
You plan your next surprise, how irrelevant
A place can be when you're there, if it isn't yours,
It's only when you get back you see what matters
And that the real truth begins and ends at home.

ENLLI

No, I've never been there, with luck never shall,
Would be bored stiff in five minutes. All islands
Of this size are horribly alike, fit only
For sheep, saints and lighthousekeepers.
I've seen it at a distance from Aber prom
And that's as near, frankly, as I want to get.
I'm not surprised that hardly anybody lives there,
The gulls' gymanfa, the endless eisteddfod of eligugs,
The drooling chatter of the tide on the pebbles,
The moronic howl of the wind—well, I ask you.
Not, you'll say, much different from what goes on
On the mainland ? Point taken. But
On top of all that, the traditions, paper flowers
Of crude fantasy, more than usually bogus
Even for this bloody country, if that's possible.
They had a king once, but he got drunk,
Well, that's kingly enough, but his crown
Was brass, he was appointed by the landlord.
And the gravestones of those twenty thousand saints
Thrown up in the age of faith by sheer ignorance—
Faith mostly spelt filth, futile pilgrimage
To no rational destination. I suppose that, really,
Is what Enlli is all about. You
My ancestors, were no fools who named it
One of the gates of heaven, outpost
Of the Kingdom of the Absurd, illogical,
Untidy, freak-out of geology, realm
Whose king had as good a title as some princes,
Almost, but not quite, nowhere, usually
Inaccessible but not always, utterly

Pointless but still marginally profitable,
Illusion, but anchored in rock.
If anybody prints this poem I'll send the price of it
To the fund to acquire Enlli for the nation.
God damn it, it *is* the Nation.

SELL-OUT

There was this film, see, the ultimate epic.
Starring at vast expense, Sir Richard ap Surd
Fresh from his triumph in *The Four Horsemen of the Acropolis*
And the versatile Irish beauty Nymph O'Maniac,
Supported by an impressive cast recruited
From all the out-of-work actors in Cardiff
And a chorus of singing sheep.
Script by the same talented team that gave us
My Soul is a Slagheap and *Bash Him with your Harp, Butty,*
Portraying with brutal realistic candour,
Suffused, of course, with gentle, wistful lyricism,
The pride, the passion, the heartbreak,
The goings-on and the gettings-up-to
Of our picturesque people, with extra dialogue
Specially lent by the Welsh Joke Museum.
It was called *The Rains of Rhondda,* so naturally
It was shot at Ebbw Vale. On the first day
The camera crew were drowned when the sewers burst,
Most of the cast were incapacitated for life
After a punch-up at the Puddlers' Arms
And the leading lady couldn't be prised apart
From the front row of the First XV.
They retreated in confusion, fantasy
As always in Wales swamped by the reality.
It was finished at last in Egypt
With the Pyramids disguised as coaltips
And the Sphinx made up to look like Lloyd George
And shown at the Lucrezia Borgia Memorial Film Festival.

Drooled the Arts Page of our National Newspaper :
It was as if Eisenstein had transcribed the Football Echo,
A triumph, a total experience, my bowels were moved.
The losses are estimated at an equivalent sum
To the entire gross national product of Outer Mongolia.

IEUAN AP IAGO
(On Pontypridd Bridge, January 1856)

The short days of winter,
The long hours at the loom,
I know every knot and splinter
Of wood in the long room
Where I and my son sit weaving,
As the shuttle flies under my hand
I think of my brother leaving
For a new life in a new land.
I read again his letter,
Each enticing paragraph :
Come where life is better
By broader waters than Taff.

Are there broader waters than Taff ?

The Bridge is old, and older
The Graig's brooding hill,
The nights grow colder
And the wind is chill,
You call to me, my brother,
From a richer, kinder earth,
And I'm torn, one way and the other,
That land, or this of my birth ?
Shall I go or stay, I ponder,
A new world beckons and gleams
By wider rivers than Rhondda
With fine gold in their streams.

There is fine gold in these streams

The short twilight shivers,
Night draws on apace,
Taff and Rhondda are rivers
That bind me to this place
And quench all restless fevers.
Here is where I belong,
My son and I are weavers,
Together we'll weave a song
That will teach all Wales to treasure
This wealth, this place we hold
And gather in its measure
The music and the gold.

> *The music and the gold.*

THE OLD LEADER

Fetch my cloth cap from the wardrobe,
My muffler and cords and yorks,
I've got to slip down to the Institute
To give one of my heartfelt talks

About the Workers and their struggle
And the brotherhood of Man,
For we've got to stave off the future
By all the means we can.

And the past will unfold its pageant
And we'll live the old glories again,
The depression, the strike, the means test,
The hunger marches and Spain.

That's the stuff that will stop them thinking
About what's happening today,
Bemuse them with lies and legends
And filch their future away.

Shine up the blue scar on my forehead,
A bluer there's not to be found.
There's lucky I was to be clumsy
The two days I worked underground.

We haven't got very much longer
To keep a tight grip on Wales,
So fetch my cloth cap from the wardrobe,
It's next to my top hat and tails.

THREE PARODIES

1 ELEGY FOR A FRIED EGG

You should have heard me the other night
Railing at shoddy materialism and the price of grub
In a phony pretentious restaurant in Queen Street
Where the soup came out of a tin and the pâté maison
Was bought at the supermarket, one of those places
Frequented by secondhand car salesmen
That fine flower of the Welsh metropolis
And their expensive kept bitches.
Christ, how I told them a thing or two, while my grandfather
Keeled over on to the cheeseboard from sheer decrepitude.
As they chucked me out I thought of Rilke,
That homosexual French dwarf who cut his ear off
And ran away to Tahiti,
I thought of Captain Cook who set sail
From the lake in Roath Park and discovered Patagonia.
I thought of Miss Pugh next door but one
And her big tits. Then I went home
And wrote a poem about a hamster
Before catching a deisel to death.

DAI DRIPP

Hubby was cleaning the mini
And I was making a flan,
Cuddles was eating her Weetybits
When suddenly I had a plan
To supplement the housekeeping
And keep up with the folks in the road
By having a bash at poetry
And running up an ode
As neat as a good-class semi,
Brisk, cheerful and bright
But with just that tough of meaning
That makes it sound all right.
Nothing deep or gloomy,
No boring political guff
But cleaning and shopping and babies,
Sensible wholesome stuff.
And I sent it to an editor
Whose name, I'm afraid I forget
But he lives in the right part of Cardiff
And I'm told he's rather a pet.
And I'm terribly glad I tried it,
And Hubby is pleased as well
For it's much more fun than knitting
And awfully easy to sell.
So, all suburban housewives
You won't find the job too hard,
Take five minutes off from the housework
And you too can be a bard.

SUSAN SPAM

One day while I was docking swedes
With a slow moronic grin
And all my ancestors' misdeeds
Wrought their sour death within.

Suddenly there came into view
A figure gaunt and tall.
He said, Forgive me naming you.
I made no sound at all.

He carried on at tedious length
About my life so grim,
It took all my idiot peasant strength
To be polite to him.

At last he ceased and strode away,
The cold Welsh rain came down,
In puddles in that barren clay
I watched my country drown.

Then, indistinguishable from mud,
I started my old car,
The sickness of my tainted blood
Inclined me to a jar.

And oh what festering itch of sin
Brought this damp thought to me
As I fuddled in a squalid inn :
Un bain't much help to we.

                              IANTO RHYDDERCH

WALDO

I had my photo taken with him once
In a pub in Pontarddulais but
Paul Riley didn't twist the spool before
Taking the next snap, the only picture
He ever spoilt. So now I have no record
Of that summer meeting.

        Yes Waldo,
It was always summer when I met you—
You are my personal Bardd yr Haf—
An eisteddfod or a conference, a froth
Of holiday and high endeavour your presence
Turned to wine. Not your rare words
You had already spoken. We gathered
Under the leaves of the tree, the light
Interpreted.

        Llangollen Bridge, not even
The tourist industry can cheapen it, but
For me it's where we first met, talked
About nothing much, made contact. I had
Nothing in common really with this
Quaker, pacifist, mystic, cywyddwr,
A better poet and a better man,
Someone I might have been like with luck
And effort, but am not. That botched snapshot
Ten years ago is the true symbol ;
Not even the best painter I've known
Could put us in the same picture.

THE ROCK AND THE BOOK

Floodlit the rock of the Gododdin floats
Above the shops and bars. Valhalla ? No,
More like the island of Laputa, incompatible
With the real world, lovely for a festival
But only scenery after all. Stick it up there,
Forget about it, they say, another people
Turning its back on their history, wallowing
In the mere present. The old city is not quite
A morgue or a museum, Deacon Brodie, Montrose,
John Knox, Mary Stewart and David Hume
Are still here, just. Feel the psychic wind
Of their passing in the Lawnmarket, or is it only
The cold air sneaking in from the sea ?
Is there anyone here at all ? Emptiness echoes
Even when there are people about. This
Is what it is like to be a former capital.
The old parliament building is closed for repairs.
Why bother ? The Turks were kinder to Athens
And the Russians to Prague. There at least
There was no pretence.

Wade through the jettisoned centuries, prod
For silted relics, read in a glass case
Letters by dead hands, archive of a dead kingdom.
Our language was spoken here once, and here
Our literature began, chanted on those ramparts
Whose magic is dependent on a switch
That can be turned off at any time.

Return

To a country whose chief city has no intrusive
Dramatic thrust of rock at its flat centre, built
Mostly on sand and mud. There in an iron box,
In an ugly building, they hide an old brown book
The colour of seaweed. You wouldn't look at it twice
Unless you knew, unless you knew.